A gift for:

_____

From:

_____

Soul Restoration: Hope for the Weary
Copyright ©2005 by Terri Blackstock
ISBN-10: 0-310-80546-5
ISBN-13: 978-0-310-80546-5

Requests for information should be addressed to:
Inspirio, The gift group of Zondervan
Grand Rapids, Michigan 49530
www.inspiriogifts.com

Associate Publisher: Tom Dean
Design Manager: Val Buick
Production Management: Matt Nolan
Design: Gayle Raymer
Editing and compilation: SnapdragonGroup Editorial Services
Cover photo: Corbis

Printed in China
05 06 07/LPC/ 4 3 2 1

MEDITATIONS FROM
TERRI BLACKSTOCK

$\mathcal{H}$OPE FOR THE WEARY

SOUL RESTORATION

inspirio™

*I*n 1995, before my first Christian novel, *Evidence of Mercy*, was published, I proofread the galleys with a bit of fear and trembling. I was zealous to reach people through my fiction, but I wasn't sure I had succeeded. There's a fine balance between telling a good story and crafting a strong message. I worked hard to weave my spiritual theme into the plot in a way that would not be overpowering to the reader. But having done so, I feared some of my readers might come away with a spiritual yearning without understanding how to make the rest of the journey.

In response to this, I decided to include what I called an "Afterword" (really an Author's Note), with some of my own spiritual thoughts. In that, I didn't have to follow the "rules" of good storytelling. It was separate and apart from the story—an example of how my own spiritual yearning was finding fulfillment in my life.

Over the years, many readers have expressed their appreciation for these honest glimpses into my personal journey. Some even tell me that when they buy one of my novels, they turn to the back of the book to read my "Afterwords" first. For that reason, I've decided to pull out some of those "Afterwords" and put them into a book of devotionals, along with some new ones that I hope will bless you.

I hope these will be a beneficial complement to your regular Bible study and prayer, an enhancement to your quiet time with the Lord. I pray that you will use them to help you ponder God's goodness and his nature. May God use them to bless you in every good way.

—*Terri Blackstock*

TABLE OF CONTENTS

*T*hough you have made me see troubles,
many and bitter,

You will restore my life again;
from the depths of the earth

You will again bring me up.
You will increase my honor

and comfort me once again.

❧

PSALM 71:20–21

This book is lovingly dedicated to the Nazarene.

ommit your way to the LORD;

trust in him and he will do this:

He will make your righteousness shine

like the dawn,

the justice of your cause like the

noonday sun.

PSALM 37:5−6

DISCOMFORT'S HIDDEN *B*LESSING

Endure hardship with us like a good soldier.

2 TIMOTHY 2:3

I hate discomfort. I'm a cushy kind of person, one who needs air-conditioning and soft carpet, the right chair to write in, a car that doesn't rattle, salty things to eat, flat shoes with rubber soles, and Diet Coke. I'm largely uncomplicated. Keep me comfortable, and I can be very pleasant. Ask me to rough it, and I might turn on you.

I pondered the comfort of my life when I began working on my Restoration Series. I wanted to write a series, set in our time, when all electronic technology in the world fails. Cars die suddenly, planes fall from the sky, the electricity goes out, along with anything that requires an electrical charge to operate. I wanted to show a

Christian family in the midst of an upper middle class neighborhood, suddenly thrust back to *Little House on the Prairie* days. I wanted to explore what might happen to a family much like mine, if all the comforts were taken from them. If they were left living in their beautiful, high-tech homes, only there were no lights or air-conditioning, no television or computer, no phones or microwaves.

Would it bring out the best or the worst in people? Would there be looting? What if people were robbing and killing for the scarce provisions—would even my Christian characters commit crimes in order to eat?

In writing the first book of that series, I tried to imagine my own family sitting in a dark house at night with only a kerosene lamp. What would we do to entertain ourselves? My own whining would rival my children's. I wondered how long it would take me to give up whining and get to work living. How long would it take me to see the blessing of discomfort?

I'd like to think it wouldn't take me long, but I know better. I've had tastes of discomfort over the past few years. A chronic back problem has given me great discomfort and become a source of much whining to God. I've spent a great deal of money, time, and energy trying to find a solution to my problem. I've prayed earnestly and often for healing. I've been prayed over and prayed for. I've done what the Bible says to do to be healed. Yet my pain, while minor, is still there, and I still manage to whine about it.

In fact, I manage to whine even when things are good. When my books are selling well and people are writing me and my publishers are sending me around the country and I'm getting speaking invitations and endorsement requests … I usually whine because I'm overworked or stressed out. And I realize that if I can't see the blessing in the good times, how on earth will I ever see the blessing in the bad?

God has a funny way of teaching me lessons through the books I write. When I first came up with the idea for the Restoration Series, I hoped I would cause Americans to think about the things that are really important in life. I hoped I would make them reorganize their priorities. I hoped that contemplating the essentials of their lives would draw them into a closer walk with Christ.

But God had a different plan. His plan was to make *me* think about what's important, make *me* reorganize *my* priorities, make *me* contemplate the essentials of *my* life, in an attempt to draw me into a closer walk with him.

He wanted me to know the blessing in discomfort. That sometimes he has to strip us down to our bare essentials in order to make us useful for his kingdom. He may strip down our technology. Turn off our air conditioners. Stall our cars.

He might allow us to face unemployment … or even bankruptcy.

He might allow us to struggle with back problems or multiple sclerosis or cancer.

Our spouse may die. We may lose a child.

We could find ourselves alone.

But even if all the trappings of our lives were gone, we would still be able to look up to him and know that the most important thing in our lives can never be taken from us. Through our crises, we find the faithfulness of a God who loves us enough to make us uncomfortable. A God who wants our lives to revolve around him, because he's the only one who can bring us true fulfillment and abundance. He alone holds the key to our true potential.

That's when he can restore us to the person he meant for us to be. The One who is unencumbered by the entanglements of the world, who understands that we are soldiers on the front lines of a spiritual war. One who knows that this is not our home, so we are never really to be comfortable here. ◁

HEAVENLY FATHER: *I don't like those uncomfortable stretches, but I do believe you can use them to strengthen and discipline me and produce character in my life. When the strong winds begin to blow and the rain begins to fall, be my shelter from the storm. Give me a glimpse of the rainbow that will one day appear at your command. I trust you, Lord. AMEN.*

Endure hardship as discipline; God is treating you as sons.... No discipline seems pleasant at the time, but painful. Later on, however, it produces a harvest of righteousness and peace for those who have been trained by it. Therefore, strengthen your feeble arms and weak knees.

HEBREWS 12:7, 11–12

JUST PASSING *THROUGH*

> [Jesus] said to me: "It is done. I am the *Alpha* and the
> *Omega*, the Beginning and the End. To him who is thirsty I
> will give to drink without cost from the spring of the water of
> life. He who overcomes will inherit all this, and I will be his
> God and he will be my son."
>
> REVELATION 21:6–7

You might say I'm delusional. I have that American virus, the one
that says that all the trappings of this world, from prosperity to
technology, from entertainment to security, from excess to extreme,
will just march along indefinitely. I have that infection that makes
me think that all this somehow has something to do with me, and
that as long as I don't mess up really badly, things will keep going
along just as they are.

When an ice storm hits my unprepared southern town, and the power lines are knocked down by tree branches heavy with ice, we leave our dark, cold houses and ride around in our cars to get warm. We drive to the homes of friends to shower, wash clothes, and mark time  waiting for the electric company to get those lights turned back on. We hold our collective breath until McDonald's is operational again and we can watch the latest reality show.

What if it never came back on? What if, in his sovereignty, God said, "That's enough. It's time for it to stop. I've tried for years to get your attention, but you won't look up. So I'm going to do something drastic to change you and make you better." He says in Isaiah 48:10, "See, I have refined you, though not as silver; I have tested you in the furnace of affliction."

What might that test look like? Might it be a massive power outage like the one in my books? Might it be hurricanes one after another, or tsunamis, or mudslides, tornadoes, or terrorists? Might it be war on our own soil?

Or might it be more personal? Something closer to home. Something that hurts from the center of our being, in that place in our gut where we never quite recover.

In the severity of that thing, whatever it might be, would we see his gentle hand? Would we see compassion from the God who loves us? Would we see his love manifested in our crisis?

And how would we change?

Would he prepare us first? Is he preparing us even now?

I'll never forget the morning that my sweet mother-in-law was in a car accident that left her with a closed head injury from which she would never fully recover. That morning, as I prayed, God prompted me to ask that I would be ready when tragedy hit, and that he would make my husband and me strong enough to sustain it when it came. Hours later, I knew why I'd prayed that prayer.

Over the next year, we watched that beloved woman suffer. She was never the same again, and spent the rest of her life in confusion and frustration, unable to do any of the things she did before, unable to even recognize her own home. She died of a secondary infection, but by the time she went, we had already said good-bye. In his gracious kindness, God had given us a year to release our hold on her, to realize that, in a way, she was already gone. In his compassion he made us ready for her passing home.

Sometimes he does that with our entanglements on earth. He tells us that this is not our home and gently teaches us that the things here are just temporary. They're not ours, anymore than the things in a European hostel are ours when we're traveling abroad. We have no ownership of that bed we slept in, or the table on which we set our things. The lamp in the corner belongs to someone else. When we return home, we will leave it behind.

The Bible says we are aliens in a land not our own, sojourners passing through, pilgrims on our way to a destination we haven't quite reached. We should look at the things in our lives as temporary pleasures, things to be grateful for, but things that we can easily leave behind.

Our gaze should be set on our real home, for we are "strangers and exiles on the earth" (Hebrews 11:13 NASB). God has prepared a city for us, and it's nothing like this one.

Sometimes the letting go is hard. We kick and scream and cry and plead with God to give it back. Our loved one who died, our good health, our home, our car, our bank account, our comfort.

But sometimes he loves us too much to do it. Sometimes his will is for us to look toward home, anxiously waiting for that day when we reach the gates of our own city. That place where all our ultimate comforts lie. That place where we will be welcomed in like dearly loved children long awaited. ◦—

DEAR LORD: *When I feel confused and out of touch with my surroundings, help me remember that my spirit is simply longing for my real home—the place you have prepared for me. I know it will be far above what I could ever imagine. I long for it. But I also know that you want me to finish my journey here on earth. Give me the strength and the courage to do that in a way that is pleasing to you, my Savior and my God.* AMEN.

God] will wipe every tear from their eyes. There will be no more death or mourning or crying or pain, for the old order of things has passed away."

REVELATION 21:4

THE POWER
OF A $\mathscr{H}$UG

> In all these things we overwhelmingly conquer through
> Him who loved us. For I am convinced that neither death, nor
> life, nor angels, nor principalities, nor things present, nor
> things to come, nor powers, nor height, nor depth, nor any
> other created thing, will be able to separate us from the love of
> God, which is in Christ Jesus our Lord.
>
> ROMANS 8:37–39 NASB

My husband, Ken, is a great hugger. His hugs offer comfort and
acceptance to everyone who's blessed to receive one from him. I
tease him, saying that people come from miles around to hug him.
That may be an exaggeration, but I do know that men and women
alike will cross our huge sanctuary for one of his special hugs.

21

The hugs he gives me, though, are even more special. With me, he doesn't quickly let go, and he always whispers something sweet in my ear, kisses my neck, and reminds me that I'm the only recipient of this unique variation of his special gift.

Returning home one night after an extended season of travel—ten trips in as many weeks—I received an unusually special hug from Ken. As I walked into his waiting arms, he pulled me close and held me so tight that I felt love seeping into every aspect of my being. That tight, lingering, desperate hug said that he loved me more than anyone else on the earth ever had and that he'd missed me terribly.

Now don't get me wrong. I know that Ken does fine when I'm away. He's a very independent man with a full, busy life. But when he told me that night that he feels incomplete without me and proved it with that hug, I believed him. I could feel that it was true.

Gratitude filled my heart, not only for my husband's love and devotion but also for what it represents. Even the best examples of human love—like the love Ken and I share—is flawed and inadequate compared to God's love. But it does serve as a marker. If our love for each other is great, how much greater must be God's love for us. If we are special to

each other, how much more special must we be to our Creator.

It made me wonder how well I'm modeling God's love to the other people in my life. Are there others besides Ken who feel so loved by me that they're filled up with gratitude for the picture it  shows them of God's love? Does my love help them to understand how special they are to him?

If I'm a vessel of God's love, an instrument through which he works in the lives of his children, am I making myself available that way? Surrendering to his love makes me vulnerable, and passing it on to others is risky business. But that's what I'm called to do.

I pray that the Lord will make all of us channels through which God's great, inexplicable love can pass to others, thus making them aware of just how precious they are to him. It is one of his highest callings. ✐

HEAVENLY FATHER: Your love is so great that it is incomprehensible to me. I can't begin to understand it. Thank you for those people in my life who model your love for me so that I might at least grasp some idea of the magnitude of it. I pray that I might be a model of your love to others in return. As always, you deserve all the glory and praise. AMEN.

God is love. Whoever lives in love lives in God, and God in him. In this way, love is made complete among us so that we will have confidence on the day of judgment, because in this world we are like him.

1 JOHN 4:16, 17

TASTE AND SEE THAT THE LORD *Is* GOOD

> When I am afraid,
> > I will trust in you.
> In God, whose word I praise,
> > in God I trust; I will not be afraid.
> What can mortal man do to me?
>
> PSALM 56:3–4

When I read about the life of David, I feel swept into the story, as if it's a well-crafted novel that keeps me on the edge of my seat. At this writing, I'm studying 1 Samuel in my Precept Bible Study Course, and I'm amazed by the discomfort God sent into David's life to prepare him to be king.

David was no stranger to discomfort. As the youngest of seven sons, he was the one relegated to caring for the smelly, dirty sheep, while his brothers did mightier and nobler things—like fighting in Saul's army. He spent his days under the glaring sun, leading the sheep to food and water, watching to make sure that they didn't wander off, protecting them from lions and bears. The only thing he had for entertainment was his harp, and during those long, boring desert days and the long, lonely nights, David spent his time getting to know his God.

When God sent Samuel to anoint him king, David and his family must have thought they'd just hit Easy Street. A shepherd boy becoming king? Who could have imagined? It must have been like winning the lottery. But God hardly had that in mind.

Yes, God blessed him by rewarding his faith with victory over Goliath. And he made him successful on Saul's battlefield, so that the people sang songs about him: "Saul has slain his thousands, and David his tens of thousands" (1 Samuel 18:7). But life was hardly comfortable.

The moment Saul began to see David's star rising, he began trying to kill him. And suddenly, instead of taking his place on the throne God had promised him, David found himself a fugitive and refugee, hiding in a cave in order to stay alive.

David must have had moments of confusion, where he looked up to the heavens and asked God if there was some mistake. If he was to be king, what was he doing scrounging for food and living in a hole in a rock?

But we don't really see that in David's story. Instead, we see the Psalms he wrote during that time, songs of praise and thanksgiving, songs declaring his trust in the God who knows how many steps away his enemy is, the God who delivers him and keeps his promises. In Psalm 34:8,10 NASB, he urges the hearers of his song to "taste and see that the LORD is good." He reminds those who hear that "they who seek the LORD shall not be in want of any good thing."

There David was, homeless, without enough food, abandoned by the people who had once exalted him, claiming that he wanted for nothing, that God was providing for him in every way. "The righteous cry out, and the LORD hears them; he delivers them

from all their troubles" (Psalm 34:17). This was something David knew to be true, and he still declares it to us today.

I take comfort from David, who had a tough life. Certainly, he brought some of his problems upon himself, but whatever his sin, and whatever his problem, he took it before God in repentance and sorrow, then trusted God's lovingkindness and forgiveness. David never expected comfort from God; he only expected deliverance.

David's time of fleeing from death, of clinging to God's protection, prepared him for the difficult task God had called him to. It made him into a man who would be the greatest king Israel ever knew, a human with failings and shortcomings, but one after God's own heart.

In my life, I've known different kinds of comfort. The kind that comes from God as I read stories like David's, and the kind that I think I need—material comforts that I've come to expect. But when the discomfort comes, through grief or tragedy or financial trials or a million other things this life brings upon me, I know where I can turn.

And I begin to long for home. ⌒

DEAR PRECIOUS FATHER: Thank you for the times when you toughen me up for the task ahead. It's difficult to see that as a kindness when I'm standing in the middle of it. But later, when I see where you have brought me and what you have helped me accomplish, my heart sings with praise and my heart bows at your feet. Help me always to be in the very center of your perfect purpose for me. AMEN.

I am like an olive tree
    flourishing in the house of God;
I trust in God's unfailing love
    for ever and ever.
I will praise you forever for what
    you have done;
in your name I will hope, for your
    name is good.
I will praise you in the presence of
    your saints.

PSALM 52:8–9

For the MOTHERS

[Jesus said,] "I have told you these things, so that in me you
may have peace. In this world you will have trouble.
But take heart! I have overcome the world."

JOHN 16:33

She came to me with her heart broken. She had just learned that her
adult daughter was badly addicted to pain killers, and it was ruining
her life. Her daughter had almost hit bottom, and she feared that the
bottom would be death itself.

Her child had been a good Christian kid, active in her youth
group. She'd gone on mission trips to help the poor and the needy.
She'd worked with underprivileged kids. She'd had lots of friends
and a bright future. And then she went away to college, and everything turned upside down.

Within a few years, her personality had completely changed. The bright light that used to surround her became a cloud of darkness and secrecy, lies and deceit. She couldn't pass her classes, lost her friends, couldn't hold a job, and made choices that would have lifelong conse-

quences. Her addiction had brought her so low that my friend doubted she would live another year unless something drastically changed. Yet she knew how little control she had. Forced treatment had little chance of working if her daughter wasn't committed to it.

She sat there weeping at the shock of it all, taking ferocious inventory of her life, trying to figure out where she had gone wrong as a mother. I suspected that it was not something she had done at all. I suspected that somewhere in her daughter's life since she'd left home, enemies had attacked and plundered and taken her daughter captive.

Not knowing what to say or do, I opened my Bible and led her to Isaiah. I wanted to show her where God says, "Can a mother forget the baby at her breast and have no compassion on the child she has borne? Though she may forget, I will not forget you! See, I have engraved you on the palms of my hands; your walls are ever before me" (Isaiah 49:15–16).

I wanted to remind her how much God loves her, and that he is in control. But then the Lord prompted me to read on, and I came to the passage that I knew God gave me for her.

"Can plunder be taken from warriors, or captives rescued from the fierce? But this is what the LORD says: "Yes, captives will be taken from warriors, and plunder retrieved from the fierce; I will contend with those who contend with you, and your children I will save" (Isaiah 49:24–25).

I knew that God was telling us that the warriors—the enemies—in her family's case, were the drugs that had imprisoned her daughter. God was saying that he could deliver her from those enemies. He could take her daughter back. And he was giving her his word that he planned to do it.

I wish I could tell you the end of the story, but it's still a work in progress. However, I do know how it will end. Her daughter will be set free, and she will be saved. God has already worked it all out somehow. I believe he led us to that passage that day, so that he could speak those words to her.

Later, as I contemplated those words, I realized that we all have fierce warriors in our lives. Whether our enemies are pride, discouragement, sickness or despair, alcohol, drugs, physical abuse, or financial crisis—God can overcome all of them. He can retrieve the plunder they've taken from us. He can contend with those who contend with us. He can save our children. And he can save us.

What a blessing to know that he has overcome the world and the trials within it, and nothing we ever face is too big for him. ❧

LORD OF GRACE AND HOPE: I offer up to you the most precious of all your gifts to me—my children. I realize the futility of thinking that I can keep them from harm in a world poised to destroy them. What comfort there is in knowing that you love them even more than I do. My arm is short, but yours is long. My understanding is small, but yours is great. I will trust in you. AMEN.

Surely the arm of the LORD is not too short to save, nor his ear too dull to hear.

ISAIAH 59:1

❧

EVERYDAY *D*ANGERS

> [God] gives strength to the weary
>> and increases the power of the weak.
> Even youths grow tired and weary,
>> and young men stumble and fall;
> but those who hope in the LORD
>> will renew their strength.
> They will soar on wings like eagles;
>> they will run and not grow weary,
>> they will walk and not be faint.
>
> ISAIAH 40:29–31

As I wrote my book, *Line of Duty*, America was preparing to go to war. Duct tape and plastic sheeting were top-selling items in the stores. Families were saying goodbye to their sons and daughters, their fathers and husbands. Yellow ribbons adorned our streetlights, trees, and fence posts. I looked ahead with uncertainty as I wrote, realizing that by the time of publication, many of you could be grieving or suffering. The potential for disaster was on the horizon. The very air we breathed could turn into poison.

But it strikes me now, looking back, that those threats were no worse than the threats I face today. One of my children could get sick and die. A drunk driver could slam into our car and destroy our family. Evil influences could direct my children into choices that will ruin their lives. Only through the power of God can I live with these daily terrors, knowing they exist, but trusting God to protect and provide. I regret that I have not always had those assurances.

For the first twenty-two years of my Christian walk, I showed up for church each Sunday and Wednesday night and sat there listening to the Word of God. The Holy Spirit would stir within me, calling me to take hold of the power and abundant life Jesus had promised me. But it seemed that doing so required too much of me. Sometimes I carried my Christianity like heavy baggage that needed to be unpacked and used. The burden weighed me down and exhausted me as I lugged it around, all the while unaware that if I opened it up and learned of its beauty, it would buoy me instead.

I knew of others who had unpacked their Christian bags, who had taken out the contents and marveled at the treasures. They wore the contents draped on their bodies like the very robes of Christ, and they didn't seem weighted down and tired. They seemed strong, empowered—eager for more. Even when trials came their way, they seemed to shine in a way that I never did. Sometimes trials descended on them, and they lost a child or a spouse, and suffered the grief those terrors brought. But even through that, they prevailed with power and strength, buoyed by the Father they knew so well. Compared to them, I seemed like a poor caricature of a follower of Christ, an actor trying to play a part.

Are you weary and empty as I was, wondering if this is all there is? Do you walk through a world full of fear and stress, hurried with busyness and problems, almost crushed with the conflicting burdens you carry? Jesus said, "Come to me, all you who are weary and burdened, and I will give you rest. Take my yoke upon you and learn from me, for I am gentle and humble in heart, and you will find rest for your souls. For my yoke is easy and my burden is light" (Matthew 11:28–30).

In this fast-paced world of terror and hatred, dread and stress, you need to know that he has so much more for you than fear

and weariness. Let him release you from that burden today, and show you what he has for you. What he can do in you and through you and with you. What he made you to be. ⌒

> DEAR FATHER: *I've been staggering under the weight of my burdens, never realizing that you have been there all along, ready to take the heaviness from my shoulders and replace it with rest and peace. I open my heart now, releasing every worry and care to your all-sufficient arms.* AMEN.

---

he LORD replied, "My Presence will go with you, and I will give you rest."

EXODUS 33:14

DIVINE *TRANSFORMATION*

*The God of all grace, who called you to his eternal glory
in Christ, after you have suffered a little while, will himself
restore you and make you strong, firm and steadfast.*

1 PETER 5:10

I married my husband, Ken, in brokenness. And in that first year, we nearly broke each other.

My first marriage lasted thirteen years—years that I thought were happy. Then, in a matter of a few weeks, my world fell apart and I found myself alone with two little girls. It hadn't been my choice, and it was mostly out of my control. But there I was, doing damage control in my children's lives and trying to survive as a single mom.

I met Ken at church when I'd been divorced for a year and a half. He was a Sunday morning self-starter, meaning no one had to drag him to church. He came alone, willingly, which led me to the assumption that he was a godly man. After a whirlwind courtship, we rushed to get married, hoping it would heal the brokenness in each of us. And then our problems began.

You see, neither of us was what we appeared to be. Though I was a Christian, I wasn't walking very closely with Christ. I was still writing secular romance novels—books with graphic sex and profanity—and that had caused a rift in my relationship with Christ. Ken had been baptized as a child, and went to church as a matter of habit. But his heart was far from the Lord.

Over that first year of our marriage, the reasons for our divorces became apparent to each of us. The banners of our weaknesses seemed to fly over the household, magnified and visible to everyone who cared to look. Pride rippled between us, and much of the time we were angry and threatening to walk out. "This just isn't working," became a common refrain. Our children—my two girls and his son—were in turmoil. And we often wondered if it was even worth it.

Then one day, about a year into our marriage, Ken had an experience. He was traveling by car, and for some reason, started

listening to Christian radio. Adrien Rogers was preaching, and something he said hit Ken right between the eyes. He pulled the car over to the side of the road and began to weep. For the first time in his life, he confessed to the Lord what a wretch he was and realized his need for a Savior. He sat there, weeping and repenting of his sins and begging Christ to change him.

When he came home that day and told me what had happened, I didn't quite know how to react. "I met the Lord for the first time today," he said.

I didn't want to hear that. Hadn't I married a Christian man? "But you told me you already knew Christ," I said.

My husband was insistent. "I've always known about him. But I've never really known him until today."

Who could argue with that?

And once I saw the transformation that took place in Ken's life, I realized that this conversion experience was real … and that it was going to save our marriage. Overnight, Ken became a new creation. Ministry became the sole focus of his life. Everywhere he went, he looked for people to tell about Jesus. He joined ministries at our church, began soaking up the Bible with a zeal I'd rarely seen, and began bearing fruit in a way I'd only read about.

Watching Ken, I began to remember the height from which I'd fallen. Years earlier, when I was a new Christian, I had been just as zealous for the Lord. But that was before I'd made my Christianity a lower priority than my own selfish desires. Since that time, I'd strayed so far from Christ that I had become completely useless to God. I didn't want to be useless anymore.

Through my husband's example, I began to realize there were things in my life that I needed to give up. My career was one of them. If I were to ever make a difference for God's kingdom—as my husband was doing daily—I would have to give up writing those graphic novels and devote my gifts to Christ. I felt God calling me to sever my ties with that part of my life and start over fresh, using my gifts for him.

I remember the fear and exhilaration I felt when making that decision. After much prayer and trepidation, I got down on my knees

and told the Lord that I never wanted to write another word that didn't glorify him. Thus began my Christian writing career and years of blessings too numerous to count.

It's been twelve years since Ken's transformation. I'll never forget how one well-meaning friend told us that Ken's zeal for Christ was charming, but it would fade in time, as that kind of zeal always did. I wish I could see that person again to tell her that it hasn't faded. It's still vibrant and alive. My husband is still in love with the Lord, and his favorite pastime is telling others about him.

DEAR FATHER: *I want every area of my life to glorify you. Convict and I will repent. Speak and I will listen. Guide and I will follow. Transform me, Lord, that my life may be a shining light to those who do not yet know you.* AMEN.

Restore us, O God;
make your face shine upon us,
that we may be saved.

PSALM 80:3

PRODIGAL *DAUGHTER*

Commit to the LORD whatever you do,
and your plans will succeed.

PROVERBS 16:3

In many ways, I could be described as a Prodigal Daughter, though I never openly or consciously rebelled against God. I was raised in church and baptized at the age of ten, but it wasn't until I was fourteen that I had a genuine experience with Christ and was saved. I walked closely with him through my teenage years. However, as I reached college age, I began to grow "lukewarm" in my faith. Though I attended church every Sunday, I drifted from God in subtle ways. I stopped praying, stopped reading the Bible, and found that my focus was more on affairs of the world than on spiritual things.

When I began writing romance novels in 1982, I struggled

with how to reconcile that with my Christianity. I dreaded seeing the covers with rogue heroes kissing the necks of half-dressed women. But the romance market seemed a good place to break in as a writer since sales of those books were skyrocketing. I told myself I would only write the clean love stories, what Harlequin and Silhouette called "sweet" romances.

When I sold my first romance novel at age twenty-five, I felt like I had arrived. I was now a bona fide author, and I intended to use my gift to make a ton of money and show all those doubters who'd laughed at my dream.

But there was one problem. My clean story didn't sell very well. In typical romance novel fashion, it was on the shelves and off again in a matter of four weeks. The book had come and gone, and no one was likely to remember it. The money wasn't all that good either.

I noticed that some of my other writer friends were doing better than I was. They were selling more copies, developing name recognition, traveling and speaking. Their fame was increasing. And there was one thing they were doing in their books that I wasn't doing in mine. They were including

those sex scenes that romance novels are known for.

So I decided to be less rigid and made a few compromises in the interest of fame and fortune. One small compromise built upon another—and another, and another. But it worked. My books began to sell better, and my name was becoming better known. Thirteen years later with thirty-two titles in print, you wouldn't have even known I was a Christian.

By the world's standards, I was a success. My books were now selling to HarperCollins, as well as other publishers, with potential for movie deals, great wealth, and lots of attention. Yet … I have never been more miserable in my life. The compromises I'd made had moved me farther and farther from Christ, and I found it difficult, if not impossible, to pray. I never read my Bible, and rarely spoke of my Savior. I was in church every week, but it did me little good.

Instead of drawing me closer to Christ, church served as a sort of scouring pad, irritating and chafing me, making me nothing but uncomfortable. The emptiness within me grew in proportion to my career success until I realized that my work had become like

a brick wall between God and me. And I was the one who had erected that barrier.

I've already told you about the divorce I went through during that time, and my subsequent marriage to Ken. I've told you about my dear Ken's amazing transformation and how God used it to convict me of my need to shed the sin in my life and give my gifts to the Lord.

Looking back on all the years that had gone before, I can't help grieving when I think of how I wasted my gifts. I had allowed myself to believe that God was blessing my career and that he must want me to write those books because he had opened all the doors. Still, I knew in my heart that I was usurping God and clinging to the reins of my life. Since that time, God has taught me many lessons.

I've learned that God never gives us a gift he doesn't equip us to use—and every gift he gives has a purpose. That purpose is always to advance his kingdom and bring him glory. If we use our gifts according to his purpose, we will always be successful.

How can we fail? As we give our gifts to God, our definitions of success will change, and we'll no longer use the world's measuring stick to gauge our progress. We'll measure it all against Christ, and his purposes, and his vision for us. ⌒

PRECIOUS LORD: *Forgive me for wasting the gifts and talents you so graciously granted to me. I lay them before you now and ask you to redeem those lost years and bless the years ahead for your kingdom and glory.* AMEN.

Excel in gifts that build up the church.

1 CORINTHIANS 14:12

MOUSE IN A *MAZE*

Show me your ways, O Lord,
    teach me your paths;
guide me in your truth and teach me,
    for you are God my Savior,
    and my hope is in you all day long.
Remember, O Lord, your great mercy
    and love,
    for they are from of old.
Remember not the sins of my youth
    and my rebellious ways;
according to your love remember me,
    for you are good, O Lord.

PSALM 25:4–8

I often think my life is much like that of a mouse in a maze. There's a plan and a path that is perfect for me, and it's not so hard to find. But I can convince myself that I have a better way— a shortcut or a more interesting route to where I'm going. Sometimes, I even think the destination I choose is better than what has been ordained for me.

I picture God standing above that maze, urging me to make the turns and twists he's planned for me, luring me this way and that, showing me open doors and nudging me past the closed ones … but so often I ignore him and go my own direction. Sometimes I kick down the doors that would keep me out of trouble, and I forge headfirst into what lies behind them. Those are the times when God must weep, then let me have my way. But when I realize it and turn back, he is there waiting.

Sometimes I return to God with the consequences my choices have cost me, consequences that have made his plan for my life more difficult. But he continues to work with me, guiding me away from the dead ends, opening the doors that will lead me to what he wants me to have. Miraculously, he takes the suffering my choices caused me, the consequences that remain, and turns them into a testimony that can help others. Instead of damaged goods, I become someone he can use.

That's the grace of a Father who loved me—a poor, igno-rant, rebellious, vagabond mouse—enough to send his Son to die so that I could master that maze once and for all. With my eyes on the cross, I don't have to bump into walls and turn in circles and backtrack through the corridors of my life. All I have to do is fol-low him. And trust.

Abundant life? You bet it is.

That's why they call that grace Amazing.

FATHER GOD: I thank you for the freedom you've given me to make my own choices. I cherish that freedom and desire to use it in ways that are consistent with your plan and purpose for my life. I know that your plan is designed to keep me safe from harm and bring me fulfillment and suc-cess in all I do. Continue to teach me to use my freedom in ways that are pleasing to you. AMEN.

I know the plans I have for you," declares the LORD, "plans to prosper you and not to harm you, plans to give you hope and a future."

JEREMIAH 29:11

RIGHTEOUS *Hearts*

Religion that God our Father accepts as pure and faultless is
this: to look after orphans and widows in their distress and
to keep oneself from being polluted by the world.

JAMES 1:27

Recently, when I was reading the book of Zechariah, something
became clear that I had not understood before. It was in chapter 7.
The people had come to the prophet and asked him to inquire of
God whether they should continue to observe the fast commemo-
rating the destruction of Jerusalem. After all, Jerusalem had been
rebuilt.

God answered the people's question with a question: Was it
for me that you fasted or was it for yourselves? Then he added an
instruction that seemed unrelated to their question.

In Zechariah 7:9–10 he says: "Administer true justice; show mercy and compassion to one another. Do not oppress the widow or the fatherless, the alien or the poor. In your hearts do not think evil of each other." The people must have frowned at one another and wondered if God had misunderstood their question. They had asked about a particular day of fasting and received a lecture about justice, compassion, and the condition of their hearts.

I've read that passage before, and it has gone right over my head. But this time, it shone in my face like a beacon illuminating my own sins. I go to God expecting a pat on the back for all the good deeds I've done, all the people I've helped, all the enemies I've forgiven, all the worship I've sacrificed my time to offer. And in response, God says: "Get real, Terri. Were you doing those things for me or for yourself?"

It's as if I look up at God and ask, "What is it you want from me, Lord?"

God answers: "I want your heart to be pure. Your good deeds amount to nothing but filthy rags if your heart isn't pure. If worshipping me is a sacrifice and your good deeds are nothing more than markings on the score sheet of your life, you still don't get it."

Like the chicken and the egg question, I guess it all comes down to what we Christians continually have to ask ourselves. Which came first—the righteous heart or the good works? Do good works give us a righteous heart, or do our righteous hearts lead us to do good works? Which would God rather see?

I know the answer, and most of you do as well. God isn't interested in a score sheet or a legalistic report card. He's already done all the work to save us. He sent his Son to die on the cross for all of our sins and demonstrate our inheritance in his resurrection.

So many times I've run myself ragged trying to do things that I believe are pleasing to God, only to realize sometime later that I've neglected my prayer life and my Bible study—in fact, I've left God out of it entirely. "Was it really for me you fasted?" God asked. That's an interesting question—and a painful one.

God must sit quietly, watching and shaking his head, wondering when I will learn.

I'm so grateful that God doesn't wash his hands of us. Instead, he asks those probing, painful questions that remind us what is important. He never stops teaching us.

May our hearts be so pure, so full of his righteousness, so Christlike, that our good deeds burst forth as acts of worship, rather than sacrifice.

And may God never stop working on me. ⌒

LORD GOD: *Forgive me for the times I've smugly done my own thing and paid no attention to what you wanted. From this day forward, I want my good deeds to follow my righteous heart—a heart that listens and obeys your commandments, a heart that is pleasing to you. AMEN.*

You do not delight in sacrifice, or I would bring it; you do not take pleasure in burnt offerings. The sacrifices of God are a broken spirit; a broken and contrite heart, O God, you will not despise.

PSALM 51:16–17

THE REARVIEW MIRROR

Forget the former things;
do not dwell on the past.
See, I am doing a new thing!

ISAIAH 43:18–19

I wish I were the kind of person who had lived life according to God's best plan for me, but my free will got in the way so many times, leaving me with a series of regrets that rear their ugly heads with hair-trigger consistency. Though I read the words that Paul wrote in Philippians 3:13-14: "Forgetting what is behind and straining toward what is ahead, I press on toward the goal to win the prize for which God has called me heavenward in Christ Jesus," I find myself constantly looking in my rearview mirror, working through the things I should have done, wondering how different things would be if I had.

I judge the paths I took and the decisions I made with the critical eye of a prosecutor determined to win a case, indicting myself, convicting, and executing all at once. I run through my parenting mistakes with the skill of a D.A. I was too lenient, too strict, spoiled them too much, deprived them of what they needed. I was naïve; I was suspicious. I let them have too much freedom, or I didn't give them enough. And then there's my divorce, and the people I've offended or hurt—or the ones I failed to validate or acknowledge. I wake up nights and file through these things in my mind, asking God how he could ever have forgiven me for any of them, when compared to so many good people I know, I'm such a wretch. How can God use a loser like me? How can he count on my lazy, slow-learning spirit?

My friend Nell has the same thoughts late at night when she lies awake on the six-inch mattress provided by the county's Department of Corrections. She's been in jail on drug charges for fourteen years, since her two little boys were young. They've grown up without their mother. If anyone has a right to regrets, she does.

She looks thirteen months ahead to the date of her release, and knows she won't be able to step right back into her family and her life. She can't get back the years her drug abuse cost her. But during the time that she's been imprisoned, she has learned of Christ's forgiveness, and has been discipled and mentored by people who love her because Christ loves her. Her faith has had time to grow deep roots, and she's become something of a missionary among her cellmates.

She looks back on the last thirteen years and thanks God for all the suffering and the lessons she's learned, for it's given her a new life and transformed her into a new person. Instead of throwing up her hands as her children grow up without her, she prays earnestly for them and shares Scripture with them on the phone and during occasional visits. Nell talks to them of the things the Lord is doing in her life. She looks forward to the day when her sons will marry and have children of their own. "I didn't get to raise my boys," she says, "but I'll be the best grandmother you've ever seen!"

Nell has learned the lessons of pressing on and not looking back. She's a poignant example for me.

The apostle Peter learned this lesson too. After the Passover meal that we often call Christ's Last Supper, Jesus looked at Peter. "Simon, Simon," he said, "behold, Satan has demanded permission to sift you like wheat; but I have prayed for you, that your faith may not fail; and you, when once you have turned again, strengthen your brothers" (Luke 22:31–32 NASB).

Peter didn't know that in just a few hours, he would betray Christ three times. But Jesus knew. Jesus had told him—before the betrayal—that he would mess up, but when he repented, it would be time to move on and fulfill his calling. Jesus didn't say, "Peter, you are going to really blow it a few hours from now. You're going to turn tail and run, and then you're going to lie through your teeth about even knowing me. And it's a shame, because you had a lot of potential, but you'll be of no use to me then." Instead, he anticipated Peter's sincere repentance, and reminded him that his calling would still be there when he came back. For two thousand years, Peter has strengthened his brothers and sisters through his writings in the New Testament and reminded us that you can't move forward if you're looking back.

I realize that God is in control of the universe. The mistakes in my past, though dramatic to me, cannot ruin God's plan beyond repair. God is sovereign, and his plans cannot be thwarted by human beings like me. He can fill in the blanks of my mistakes, teaching my children what I failed to teach, restoring what I destroyed, rebuilding what I tore down, redeeming what I sold away.

The Bible tells me to stop looking back, to press on toward the prize. God knew my mistakes before I ever made them, yet he planned to use me anyway. He didn't see me as The Great Loser, but as someone uniquely gifted with something of use to his kingdom work. Where I see myself as a disappointment, he sees me as an asset. He already knows the fruit I will bear for him, and my future is on his mind, so much more than my past.

If God can see me that way, why wouldn't I want to press on toward that goal and wave goodbye to my fragmented, imperfect past? The future is so much brighter in Christ, and I have so many sisters and brothers who need strengthening.

Thank you, Lord, for seeing my potential instead of my past.

HEAVENLY FATHER: *I'm so grateful that your power and authority are so much greater than my mistakes. As I press forward, leaving my past behind, I pray that you will strengthen and establish me in the purpose for which you have called me.* AMEN.

As high as the heavens are above the earth,
    so great is [God's] love for those who fear him;
as far as the east is from the west,
    so far has he removed our
    transgressions from us.

PSALM 103:11–12

HIS HEART WAS *B*ROKEN

[The LORD says,]
"I will repay you for the years the
locusts have eaten."

JOEL 2:25

"Why do people always let you down?"

One of my children asked this question after her heart had been broken, and I wanted to leap to the defense of the human race. "They don't always let you down," I wanted to say. "Some people are reliable and dependable. Some people are good and won't hurt you."

But I stopped myself, realizing that this could be one of the greatest life lessons she would ever learn. The truth is, every human on the face of the earth has the ability to let someone down. Everyone is capable of breaking a heart. It's our nature. There is no one who can live up to another's expectations 100 percent of the time.

No one but Christ.

So I told my child that we are not to put our hopes in people, but in Christ, who would never, ever let us down.

To some people, that's good news.

To others, it's like saying we can count on the tooth fairy. To them, Christ seems so far removed from reality that they think reaching for him would be like reaching for thin air.

But they would be wrong.

You see, Jesus knows of our heartbreaks. His heart was broken when his disciples scattered to avoid arrest and one of his twelve closest friends betrayed him for thirty pieces of silver. His heart was broken when he heard that Peter, one of his most trusted confidants, had sworn he didn't even know him. His heart was broken when he hung on that cross between thieves and heard the soldiers mocking him and knew he had done nothing for which he should be executed. His heart was broken when the thief on the cross next to his cursed him and heaped insults on him. At the same time, his broken heart must have reminded him why he was there. He had come to earth for the sins that caused all of those heartbreaks.

Because of Christ's suffering, he not only understands our suffering, but he has such an affinity with us that he can call us brothers and sisters. To me, that's wonderful news! That tells me that no matter who breaks my heart in this life, or who lets me down or deceives me or rejects me or betrays me … I'll still have an anchor. Jesus understands, and he will never break my heart.

I've had heartbreaks in my life, times when I've lain in bed, hugging my knees up to my chest, weeping and hurting like I'd never hurt before. There is no hurt like abandonment or rejection. But it's my nature not to wallow in pain. I tend to do it for just a little while, then my heart bounces back, and hope springs up again. Maybe tomorrow things will get better. Maybe something good will happen. Maybe God will answer my prayer.

I think, as a Christian, I can hope like that, even in the midst of my pain, because I know that the Lord is in control. He can change the course of history. He can heal wounds. He can return the years that the locusts ate.

In my life, the locusts have done plenty of damage, but God has been faithful to undo it or make something useful out of it. It's funny how those chewed up crops sometimes turn into extravagant feasts when God starts stirring them around.

Oh, if you don't know him, what joy you are missing! Let his suffering and heartbreak change your life today. Accept the love he offered you when he gave his life for you. Focus your life on him, and he will never let you down.

PRECIOUS LORD: *Your heart was broken for me, and yet you love me still. It doesn't seem possible—a miracle called "grace." My greatest desire is that I would never again do anything to break your heart. Give me a tender conscience—one that will spring into action when I make an unwise choice or head down a road to ungodliness. Help me as I set forth to please you in everything I do and say.* AMEN.

In bringing many sons to glory, it was fitting that God, for whom and through whom everything exists, should make the author of their salvation perfect through suffering. Both the one who makes men holy and those who are made holy are of the same family. So Jesus is not ashamed to call them brothers … He had to be made like his brothers in every way, in order that he might become a merciful and faithful high priest in service to God, and that he might make atonement for the sins of the people. Because he himself suffered when he was tempted, he is able to help those who are being tempted.

HEBREWS 2:10–11, 17–18

GOD'S WORD

*Jesus answered, "It is written: 'Man does not live on bread
alone, but on every word that comes from the mouth of God.'"*

MATTHEW 4:4

I love to read, which is probably why I love to write. But lately, I've
been increasingly concerned that some readers spend hours a day
reading novels, and little or no time reading God's Word. Yes, I want
to build my readership, and I want readers to like what they read. I
have a message in my books and want that message to get into as
many hands as possible. I am also sometimes forced to measure my
success by the number of people who buy my books. If no one buys
them, the bookstores will stop carrying them. This process makes it
easy for me to get my focus off of my true purpose—which is to
point you to Jesus Christ.

If the only spiritual education you get is through one of my books, then I have failed. It isn't enough for me to point and have you give God a cursory nod. If you aren't drawn to his Word through reading mine, then I have no business writing books. And you have no business reading them.

I don't mean to sound harsh, but the Lord has been working on me about what I'm doing and why. So often, we Christians soak up messages and ideas, and sometimes we even come under conviction, and wince a time or two. But then we forget and move on to the next stimulus.

Yes, I try to pass along the hard lessons God has taught me, and I try to convey truth as the Lord has revealed it. But if you read my work and accept what I say without comparing it to the true Word of God, then you are an excellent candidate for false teaching. I am only a sister traveling the same road as you, learning lessons just like you learn them, grappling with the same growing pains, the same fires, the same trials. I have only one source for truth, and that does not lie in anyone's novel, or anyone's devotional book, or anyone's sermon, no matter how clever or eloquently written. It lies only in Scripture, which is "living and active and sharper than any two-edged sword" (Hebrews 4:12 NASB).

I do believe that God sometimes speaks to my readers through my books, that he sometimes uses me to impart messages to you. But the Holy Spirit can only do that if I'm getting out of his way, emptying myself and offering myself as a vessel to be used by him. I can tell you, that's no easy task for me. As I agonize over the words and the plots and the characters, it's easy to lose sight of the truth God wants me to pass along.

So don't trust my words—trust God's. Study the Bible—the book he has given us so we won't be swayed by any false teaching. Know his Word inside and out, so that no one can deceive you. Then, and only then, read a novel or devotional or doctrinal text, and see if you agree with the human author who's walking the same road as you, and for whose sins Christ hung on a cross and died. And when you and I are sitting side by side at the wedding feast of the Lamb, you'll see that I got there the same way you did: through believing the Word of God and acting on it.

DEAR FATHER: I have a lot to say—words are my business. Remind me often that my words have little or no value except when they guide others to your Word—the Bible. When I begin to think of myself as a success, remind me that true success is not measured by the praise of others, monetary rewards, or even personal satisfaction. It's based on eternal results—lives restored, hearts healed, individuals living in eternal relationship with you. Thank you, Lord, for letting me invest my words in life and truth rather than fame and fortune. AMEN.

---

he word is near you; it is in your mouth and in your heart," that is, the word of faith we are proclaiming: That if you confess with your mouth, 'Jesus is Lord,' and believe in your heart that God raised him from the dead, you will be saved.

ROMANS 10:8–9

My Soul Is RESTORED

The LORD is my shepherd, I shall not be
in want.
He makes me lie down in green
pastures,
he leads me beside quiet waters,
he restores my soul.

PSALM 23:1–3

Last night as I was trying to relax and fall asleep, I began reflecting on the 23rd Psalm and all the riches layered in that passage. Then I came to the phrase I've repeated and read many times before.

He restores my soul.

Always before, I had been drawn to the verse before it about how he leads me beside the quiet waters. That is, after all, a wonderful thought in such a stressful, noisy world. And I've pondered the verse after it that assures me the Lord guides me in paths of righteousness. That's particularly important to a person like me who has no sense of direction.

But this is the first time I've lingered on the thought that he restores my soul.

And he does, of course, in such a merciful way. He has restored my soul when it's been beaten and bruised by my careless actions and terrible choices. He has restored my soul when I've allowed it to run on empty. And he's restored it when I've filled it up with things it was never meant to hold. He has restored my soul when others have crushed it. He has restored it when there seemed to be no hope for restoration.

I couldn't help wondering what my life would look like if I had not allowed that restoration. What if I had pushed God away when he reached down for me like a daddy reaching for his toddler? What if I had not reached up to him, allowing him to lift me? What if I had not laid my head on his shoulder?

Where would I be if I'd had to take the punishment I deserved for the

sins I committed, and what if I'd had to walk through life without his perfect, self-sacrificing love? What if I'd had to face a future eternity with only hopelessness and fear?

Thank God for Jesus Christ, who loved me so much that he took that punishment for me, cleaned my slate, restored my soul.

I can't wait to see him face-to-face.

DEAR LORD: How grateful I am that I can place my battered and bruised soul in your mighty hands and it will be healed and restored. I need that to happen every day. What a good and faithful and discerning Father you are. I praise you for you have redeemed me and made me your own. Lead me beside still waters and into green pastures, I pray. Keep your hand on me and restore my soul. AMEN.

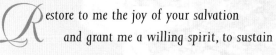

Restore to me the joy of your salvation and grant me a willing spirit, to sustain me.

PSALM 51:12

So Many QUESTIONS

Praise be to the God and Father of our Lord Jesus Christ,
the Father of compassion and the God of all comfort,
who comforts us in all our troubles, so that we can comfort
those in any trouble with the comfort we ourselves
have received from God.

2 CORINTHIANS 1:3–4

I don't understand suffering. This past year has been a time of grief for my family and many of my friends, and if I could, I would make it go away. But I can't.

At this writing, I'm grieving over the death of Landon Von Kanel, my daughter's eighteen-year-old friend, who was killed in a car accident. Just two years ago, we buried another of my daugh-

ter's friends, Anthony Shams—just 16 years of age. Both of these young men had circles of influence that reached around the globe. Their unique and vibrant personalities, colorful wit, and big dreams, made them unforgettable and irreplaceable. I daresay that thousands have been impacted by their lives and by their deaths—many for eternity. Still … I don't understand why Randy and Cindy, or Deborah and Al had to bury their children.

My friend Rick McMahan died a year ago. He was a mentor and friend to my husband and me. He and his wife, Lynda, were a true brother and sister to us. I miss seeing him on Wednesday nights after church leaning on the visitor's booth as he waited for his wife and daughter to come down from youth group. He was the one I always gravitated to when I needed to air my latest complaints about children or parenthood or life. He always seemed so in tune with God, and his wisdom always challenged me.

I miss Rick on Sunday mornings too. He and his family used to sit behind us, worshiping the Lord and shedding tears over God's goodness and awesome sovereignty. I miss Rick on Sunday nights, when we would sit together and worship again, sharing

stories and laughter and praises afterward. I miss his sense of humor and his hugs and the peace he radiated. I miss the fact that my youngest child will not be able to attend Rick's Sunday school class and experience the love he had for the kids to whom he ministered. And I miss the way Rick and Lynda's marriage set an example of love and protection and nurturing and endurance for the rest of us.

I don't know why God chose to take Rick so early, or why he allowed him to suffer as cancer ravaged his body. I don't know why Lynda and his children, Carrie and Brad, had to say good-bye to their husband and father.

I have also grieved for Stephanie Whitson, another Christian writer, who said good-bye to her husband, Bob, after a long, exhausting struggle with cancer. In his last days, when he could barely sit up, Bob searched through his Bible for reasons that we suffer and wrote it all down. This long list of possible reasons why God allows adversity to touch our lives has blessed my friend Lynda as she has grieved and suffered over Rick's death. It has also blessed many, many others. And his love and urgency to help others better understand the Lord's ways will live on long after him.

Yet Stephanie has a hole in her life, and she and their children miss him terribly.

I have grieved with my friend Patricia Hickman, another Christian writer who is completely sold out to the Lord. She and her husband, Randy, have devoted their lives to planting churches and drawing people into a knowledge of Jesus Christ. Why, then, did they suffer the loss of their beautiful twenty-year-old daughter, Jessi, in another terrible car accident? I have so many questions for the Lord, so many whys as I weep for what can never be replaced. With a daughter almost the same age, who has the same goals and interests as Jessi, I find myself shaken and humbled and slightly frightened by the suddenness of death. And my heart is broken for this dear family.

But I see so much fruit that has sprung up from these deaths and know that entire crops are yet to come. And I can't help remembering that my own salvation was the result of the death of

a boy in my school, Ricky Boggan, a fifteen-year-old who died in an accident on the way home from school. Whatever fruit I bear is his fruit too. And despite the sorrow his death produced in me as a fourteen-year-old seeker,

I am glad that God used it to bring me to him. I know the Lord well enough to trust that he is doing the same to many others as the result of these deaths.

Psalm 116:15 says, "Precious in the sight of the LORD is the death of his saints." I know this is true, and I also know that Jesus weeps over our losses and shares our grief. He also knows the future and sees the whole picture. He knows why Landon and Anthony and Rick and Jessi and Bob were called to heaven so soon. And he's already seen the reunions that are yet to come. Joyful, overwhelming, celebratory reunions.

Our God has plans and purposes that are far beyond our understanding. Sometimes those plans and purposes break our hearts. Sometimes they require sacrifices we never agreed to make. Sometimes they stop us dead in our tracks, turn us upside down, inside out, and paralyze us with pain.

But God's comfort is never far behind. As we climb up into his lap and weep into his chest, he lovingly whispers, "Shhh. Just hang on to me. I promise to see you through this. And some day it'll be clear. Remember, it won't be long until you'll see them again and you'll be together for eternity."

Our whys are rarely answered, but we trust that there is a reason. God is in control, and he loves us through our pain.

As the song says, "Life is hard, but God is good." How precious is that goodness, and how sufficient is his comfort. And how thrilling are his promises of what will happen when he returns for us.

Come quickly, Lord Jesus!

written in 2002

DEAR LORD: From the depths of my broken, fainting heart, I cry out to you. I hurt, Lord. Every fiber of my being is aching and contorting with pain. I want to run away, to escape, but my pain follows me everywhere. It invades my sleep and torments my wakefulness. I have nowhere to hide, no place to turn—but to you. Help me, Lord. Take me in your arms and wrap me up in supernatural peace. Quiet the flood of questions that are crashing over my mind. Give me rest. I place myself in your care. AMEN.

In this you greatly rejoice, though now for a little while you may have had to suffer grief in all kinds of trials. These have come so that your faith—of greater worth than gold, which perishes even though refined by fire—may be proved genuine and may result in praise, glory and honor when Jesus Christ is revealed.

1 PETER 1:6–7

The Highways to Zion

Trust in the LORD with all you heart
and lean not on your own
understanding;
in all your ways acknowledge him,
and he will make your paths straight.

PROVERBS 3:5–6

There are times when I read a passage of Scripture, and it goes right over my head. Later, the Lord will direct me to the same passage again, and it's as if one verse is framed in neon, and takes on a whole new meaning that applies perfectly to my life at that moment. I guess that's why the Bible says: "The word of God is living and active and sharper than any two-edged sword" (Hebrews 4:12 NASB).

Recently, that happened to me as I was reading Psalm 84. In the *New American Standard Bible,* Psalm 84:5 says: "How blessed is the man whose strength is in You, in whose heart are the highways to Zion!" I had been studying about the cities of refuge, and what they mean to us as Christians, so this verse took on special meaning.

Are the highways to Zion in my heart? I wondered. Do all of my roads take me to Christ? Do all my desires, all my thoughts, all my emotions, all my intentions point me to him? Have I put obstacles in my own way, roadblocks that make me stumble? Are there potholes I haven't repaired? Do I have detours that take me off that road?

I was further intrigued by the thought that the Lord didn't say that the fastest one to Zion wins, or that I had to move down that highway in a certain type of vehicle, or that my journey would be compared with anyone else's.

God simply blesses us when our hearts have the highways that take us to him!

I contemplated that for a while, and joyfully understood that the moment I surrendered my life to Christ, those highways were in my heart, already smooth and paved, and all of them took me to Christ. It is my job to keep them clear and well-maintained, to make sure they're not compromised by obstacles or unexpected pitfalls. It's my job to stay on that road. And if I ever do take a detour, I can repent, turn myself around, and get right back on the highway.

Don't we serve a remarkable Lord? He blesses us just for walking in his direction.

I pray that you will have the highways to Zion in your heart, and that every single road in your life will move you closer to Almighty God. He is eager to help you on your journey and stands waiting for you with open arms when you reach your destination!

HEAVENLY FATHER: Thank you for placing highways in my heart, smooth, strong, well-defined surfaces that lead me straight to you. It seems like an impossibility that I would ever veer off in another direction when you have set things out so well for me, but I know that I'm easily distracted. Keep your hand on me, Lord. When I go astray, place obstacles and roadblocks in my way until I come to my senses and come running back to you. I love you, Lord. AMEN.

*N*ot that I have already obtained all this, or have already been made perfect, but I press on to take hold of that for which Christ Jesus took hold of me. Brothers, I do not consider myself yet to have taken hold of it. But one thing I do: Forgetting what is behind and straining toward what is ahead, I press on toward the goal to win the prize for which God has called me heavenward in Christ Jesus.

PHILIPPIANS 3:12–14

THE POWER OF
THE CHURCH

God's household, which is the church of the living God,
the pillar and foundation of the truth.

1 TIMOTHY 3:15

Don't you hate it when things change? I sure do. And at this writing,
I'm looking ahead to a spiritual time of change. You see, my pastor,
Dr. Frank Pollard, announced this week that he will be retiring in just
a few months.

As I sat in my pew and listened to that announcement, I found
myself struck by grief, as if a family member were saying goodbye.
Selfishly, I mourned the fact that such a stable, humble, precious part
of my spiritual life would be moving on. I mourned for myself, and
wanted to cling and cry and ask him not to go. I wanted to run to

him and ask, "What about me?" But I couldn't speak at all, so I swallowed back my tears and decided to speak to him another time, when I could be less selfish and think, instead, of all that God has in store for us as our church turns this corner.

I didn't realize how important this man was to my life, since his work in this mega church made it impossible for frequent one-on-one contact with him. He had his hands full with eight thousand sheep. But more than ten years ago, when I joined his church as a broken, grieving, divorced mother of two, Frank Pollard's flock embraced me and drew me in. His philosophy was that church should be a healing place, not an execution chamber. He said time and time again, that when hurting people came to our church, we would send an ambulance and not a firing squad. In the triage of that wonderful place, my wounds were bound, and my broken heart was healed. I was able to rediscover Christ there, because he smiled at me from the faces of the members and touched me through their hands. Through Frank Pollard's two weekly messages, I grew in my walk with the Lord. His prayers and those of his flock unleashed God's power on my life as I gave my career—my last holdout—to the Lord.

So if my books have ministered to you, then you owe Frank Pollard too.

But this is not about one man. This is about the power of the church. I often get letters from Christians who aren't plugged in, and don't have that support system, that accountability, that love. Some belong to dead churches where that kind of support and ministry don't really exist. They praise God alone  from barren places, and don't know the joy of assembling together with other believers, belonging to a family to whom they can turn in times of joy and stress and devastation. They don't know the joy of being challenged by a preacher who calls them to a closer walk with Jesus.

I pray that God will lead those Christians to a new church, one where the Holy Spirit is evident as soon as they enter the building and his power is at work in the ministries. I pray that they will become involved and active. And I pray that they will experience the joy of riding in a spiritual ambulance that goes to the hurting world and tells them that healing can be found in Jesus Christ, and that he's waiting to give it to them, if only they'll open their hearts to him.

God was so good to give Frank Pollard to our church as a minister of his love. May each of you find a shepherd like him, to lead you toward the Great Shepherd. ᴄ⌐

written in 2001

DEAR LORD GOD: I thank you for my church, for those who worship next to me each Sunday. Thank you for giving me these loving souls to walk alongside me on my journey through life. They aren't perfect, Lord, but neither am I. Together we acknowledge our weaknesses and take hold of your strength. Together we are strong, because you rise up strong among us each time we gather. Bless those you've called to minister to us. Keep truth and faithfulness ever before their eyes. I thank you for them. AMEN.

The elders who direct the affairs of the church well are worthy of double honor.

1 TIMOTHY 5:17

WHEN THE SMOKE *CLEARS*

> [Jesus said,] "I am the vine; you are the branches:
> If a man remains in me and I in him, he will bear much
> fruit; apart from me you can do nothing."

JOHN 15:5

What matters to God? This question haunts me sometimes when I wake up in the night, my To-Do list reeling through my head, chiding me and reminding me that I can't possibly accomplish all I need to. My attempts to prioritize only frustrate me and set me up for failure. Could all these tasks really be that important to God? How do I sort through them and decide which tasks have eternal value, which will advance his kingdom, and which will only divert me from God's perfect purpose for me?

I ask these questions often, because when I was a Christian writing secular romance novels, I compromised like crazy by putting things in the books that would make them more marketable. I traded my Christian integrity for higher sales. I failed to glorify God in any way, and even became a stumbling block for my readers. My sales increased, all right. I appeared to be a success, but I became more miserable with every single book. I sat at my computer each morning deep in thought, Who cares how much I accomplish today? Who cares what happens to these characters? Who will care when this book is finished and it's off the shelves and nobody remembers it? What difference will all this work make?

Consider what Paul says in 1 Corinthians 3:8–15: "The man who plants and the man who waters have one purpose, and each will be rewarded according to his own labor. For we are God's fellow workers; you are God's field, God's building. By the grace God has given me, I laid a foundation as an expert builder, and someone else is building on it. But each one should be careful how he builds. For no one can lay any foundation other than the one already laid, which is Jesus Christ. If any man builds on this foundation using gold, silver, costly stones, wood, hay or straw, his work will be shown for what it is, because the Day will bring it to light. It will be revealed with fire, and the fire will test the quality of each man's work. If what he has built survives, he will receive his reward. If it is burned up, he will suffer loss; he himself will be saved, but only as one escaping through the flames."

That passage helps me put things in perspective, because it tells me that some of us will have works that remain and some of us will not. It has little to do with what the world thinks of us, or whether we've reached our specific goals, made a lot of money, or worked in a lot of ministries.

I picture myself standing before God on the day I die and enter heaven, and suddenly all the works I've done in my entire life are put into this great big pile. All of it, good and bad, everything that I've done, whether it's lasting or not—all of it dumped into that pile. Everything I thought had meaning on earth, everything I

worked hard to accomplish, every business transaction, every conversation, every dollar I spent, every action I took, every position I served, every committee I chaired, every meeting I attended, every trip I took, all

stacked there in front of me.

I stand there feeling satisfied because my pile of works is so big. As they dump my books into the stack, I smile and pat myself on the back. Look at all that work. Isn't God proud? The stack will get higher because of those junior high kids I hosted in my home. That's got to be worth something. And that kid I used to pick up and take home on Wednesday nights should count for a lot. I stayed late and cleaned up after the prayer conference. The pile grows even higher.

But then something happens—my pile is on fire. I start to back away, avoiding the heat as the flames begin to consume my works. The books are burning, but not just the secular ones. My Christian books are burning too. They're all being tested with fire. Every page of every book is going up in flames. Alarmed, I look around, wondering if this is a mistake. Didn't they count? I know God wanted me to write them. He seemed pleased with me when I did.

All the trash I picked up after the prayer conference is burning, along with the notes I took and the appointments I kept. Then I notice my day planner, which proves I

worked hard for the Lord. It's all going up in flames.

The pile begins to shrink as the works burn up, and all my efforts turn to ashes. The smoke billows up, filling the room. I can barely even see through it. I squint my eyes, holding my breath, waiting to see what will really remain when the flames die and the smoke clears. Through the haze, I strain to see what's left. Has anything remained?

And then I see him—a man walking through the ashes. I've never seen him before, but he comes through the smoke with a poignant smile on his face, and thanks me for writing books that led him to Christ. Then I see a woman who tells me she repented of some things after reading one of my books, and accepted my challenge to produce more kingdom fruit in her life. I see a group of teens who gave their lives to Christ after a youth conference I supported financially. I see the smile on the face of the bereaved widow who ate the meal I took her.

But there are more. A crowd emerges through that smoke, people I've never heard of and never touched in any way. There are hugs among the people in the crowded room, laughter and jubilation.

And then I realize who they are.

These are the people who were touched by the people I touched.

Matthew 10:41 NASB says: "He who receives a prophet in the name of a prophet shall receive a prophet's reward; and he who receives a righteous man in the name of a righteous man shall receive a righteous man's reward."

So if I spur someone to win souls, those souls will be counted among my works? I'll receive the same reward as the person who shared Christ with them? The tangible results of my work will be gone—all those pages, all those characters, all those appointments, all those trips. But the impact they had on people's hearts will still remain.

What if we thought of that pile of works every time we encountered a demand for our time? If we imagined which things might have eternal value, would we do them? Would it clear our desks?

So now, each time I face a demand for my time, I wonder …

If I do this …

Who will be there when the smoke clears?

DEAR LORD: *I want to bear much fruit for your kingdom. I want to invest my life in what will last when the flames die and the smoke clears. Guide my hands; direct my feet; open my eyes. Make me an extension of yourself as you reach out to a lost and hurting world. Then and only then will I know that my works will remain.* AMEN.

How, then, can they call on the one they have not believed in? And how can they believe in the one of whom they have not heard? And how can they hear without someone preaching to them? And how can they preach unless they are sent? As it is written, "How beautiful are the feet of those who bring good news!"

ROMANS 10:14–15

IT'S ALL ABOUT COVENANT

*For this reason a man will leave his father and mother and be
united to his wife, and they will become one flesh.*

GENESIS 2:24

❈

This weekend I married off my firstborn child. If you've ever been
the mother of the bride, you understand the exhaustion that is taking
hold of me today, setting into my muscles like the fingers of an
angry masseuse. You understand the distraction with details that
could cause you to spray your hair with bug repellant and brush
your teeth with hemorrhoid cream. You understand swollen feet
and blisters on your calluses. And that sad, anemic bank account
that will take years to recoup.

And you understand the emotions hitting you from every side, knocking you senseless. Weddings are not for the faint of heart.

I planned this wedding with the hope of having a sacred, serious ceremony as my daughter and her fiancé made this covenant together. I dreamed of having meaningful things to say to her before she went down the aisle, praying with her and kissing her good-bye. Instead, I was swept into the chaos of pictures and makeup and family and guests and more pictures and the tornado warning and the pounding rain and more pictures. I imagined myself weeping through the ceremony, but instead I sat on that front row wishing someone would straighten the train on my daughter's gown, hoping the guests didn't notice the wrinkles in her dress, hoping her new shoes didn't get tangled up in her hem. I've often wondered why more mothers of the bride don't cry when they see their daughters come down the aisle. Now I know!

In the days leading up to the ceremony, I tried to think of ways to make this wedding a witness for Christ. How could we put the focus on him? How could we

make the guests understand what each tradi-
tion meant to us? At first, I planned to set up
stations at the reception, with explanations
of the various covenant traditions. I wanted
to write those explanations, have someone do them in calligraphy,
have them matted and framed. But how did you get a thing like
that done with all the million other details that had to be handled?

I wound up writing it all out, and putting it into a program
booklet to hand out to the guests as they came into the ceremony.
I imagined they would read it as they waited for the ceremony to
start, getting into the spirit of worship, and that they could take it
home for a keepsake.

But the guests didn't get them as they came in, and at the
last minute, someone passed them out—too late for most of the
guests to read them. I have a feeling most of them were tossed
into a trash can or trampled underfoot.

So in case you're interested in what the wedding traditions
mean to my family and me, I'll include it here. Maybe it will
mean something to you. Maybe you can use it in your daughter's
wedding. Maybe it can still be a witness for Christ.

WHAT THE WEDDING
TRADITIONS MEAN TO US

THE COVENANT

In biblical times, a covenant was entered when two parties split an animal in half and walked between the pieces, symbolically saying, "May God, who witnesses this agreement, do to me what he has done to this animal, if I break this covenant." When God made his covenant with Abraham in Genesis 15, he went between the pieces as a smoking oven and a flaming torch. In essence, he took responsibility for both sides of the covenant, offering his life if the covenant was broken. This set the stage for the redemption that God would offer in the person of Jesus Christ when generations of men broke God's covenant. God himself came to earth as a baby, in the person of Jesus Christ, for the sole purpose of dying on the cross for our sins, so that we might be reconciled to him.

The bride's walk between friends and family, who witness their covenant, and the bride and groom's recessional between the people, are symbols of that sacred ceremony.

We ask you to witness this profound promise between these two, and encourage and pray for their marriage, that they may keep the sacred vows that they are exchanging.

THE EXCHANGE OF THE RINGS

The rings, which are a perfect circle, symbolize the duration of this covenant: as long as both the bride and groom live. But they also symbolize an ancient custom of exchanging possessions at the institution of a covenant. In the Bible, Prince Jonathan and David, the shepherd boy, exchanged robes as they entered a covenant. The exchange symbolized the two becoming one, and after that, if David wore Jonathan's robe, he was seen not as a shepherd, but as a prince. The two were sworn to protect each other and their families for as long as they lived.

The process of exchanging rings is also a symbol of two becoming one. When that ring is put on the fourth finger of the left hand (the finger once believed to have an artery that goes straight to the heart), the giver of the ring is saying, "I give you everything I own, and you will have every privilege I have, as well as my love, and my protection for the rest of my life."

The Exchange of the Vows

The vows remind us of the wedding to come between Christ and his bride, the church, our greatest model of what an earthly marriage should be. In Ephesians 5:24–31, husbands are told to love their wives as Christ loved the church and gave himself up for her, and wives are told to submit to their husbands as the church submits to Christ. Notice Paul says in verses 28 and 29, "In this same way, husbands ought to love their wives as their own bodies. He who loves his wife loves himself. After all, no one ever hated his own body, but he feeds and cares for it." The vows are the unbreakable promises the couple makes in their covenant to become one, witnessed by friends, family, and God himself. "What … God has joined together, let no man separate" (Matthew 19:6 NASB).

The Unity Candle

The lighting of the Unity Candle symbolizes two individual persons dying to themselves and uniting into one light with a new purpose, new responsibilities, and new privileges. "For this reason a man will leave his father and

mother and be united to his wife, and the two will become one flesh" (Ephesians 5:31).

THE EXCHANGE OF NAMES

In the Old Testament, when God made a covenant with his people, he changed their names. Abram became Abraham, Sarai became Sarah, and Jacob became Israel. Covenant partners throughout history would join names to symbolize their covenant. Today, when two are joined in marriage, the woman takes the man's name to signify that this covenant has been made.

THE EXCHANGE OF CUPS

In biblical times, a man who wanted to marry a woman would first ask his own father. If he approved, the groom's father would approach the father of the woman, and ask for her hand. The two fathers would negotiate a proper price for the bride, because she was very valuable to her family. Once they came to an agreement and gave their blessings, the groom would then offer a cup to the woman and say, "Will you take this cup?" If the woman drank of the cup, she was accepting the proposal.

At Jesus' last supper, he broke from the Passover tradition, and said, "This cup is the new covenant in my blood, which is poured out for you" (Luke 22:20). In offering the cup to his disciples, he was entering a covenant with them, a covenant that would be forged in his own blood. When the disciples drank of that cup, they were accepting that covenant—a covenant that would cost most of them their earthly lives, though they gained eternal life. In drinking of the cup, they were vowing to spend the rest of their lives serving the covenant. Today, Christians celebrate communion, drinking the cup as a reminder of the covenant they, too, have entered with Christ, and reminding them of their responsibility to serve this covenant for the rest of their lives.

Today, when the bride and groom exchange cups at the reception, they are in the same way reaffirming the covenant they have just made, again proclaiming that the two are becoming one, never to be separated again.

THE EXCHANGE OF CAKE

As the bride and groom fulfill the tradition of feeding the cake to each other, they are once again symbolizing the concept of "two becoming one." At Jesus' last supper, he held up the bread and said that it was his body. As the disciples ate of it, they again accepted the covenant, symbolically taking Jesus into themselves, becoming one with him. As the bride eats the groom's cake, and the groom eats the bride's, they are doing the same, symbolizing, "What is mine is yours, what is yours is mine."

THE COVENANT MEAL

In ancient times, when a covenant was made, it was celebrated with a covenant meal, and all of the witnesses and parties of that covenant would share in a feast together. We invite you to our wedding reception, to join in the celebration of the covenant you have just witnessed. ᴄ—

DEAR FATHER: Help me to always understand that the moment I gave my life to you, I entered a covenant with you. Help me to live in light of that covenant, serving you as your faithful bride. AMEN.

Carefully follow the terms of this covenant, so that you may prosper in everything you do.

DEUTERONOMY 29:9

INTO HIS *ARMS*

Praise be to the Lord, to God our savior,
who daily bears our burdens.

PSALM 68:19

Even though I've been blessed with a life fairly free of major crises, I seem to live each day with a sense of trepidation, waiting for the other shoe to drop. Knowing that Christian people are not immune to tragedy, I seem to brace myself, waiting for it to come.

And even as I do, I know that blessings often come through crises. I prepare for that time when my heart will be broken, praying that I'll have the strength I've seen in some of my friends when their time of mourning has come, and knowing that the promise of Romans 8:28 will stand. "In all things God works together for the good of those who love him, who have been called according to his purpose."

Sometimes a crisis can sneak up on you—like guerilla warriors planning their ambushes behind walls and bushes. At this writing, I'm dealing with my daughter's illness—a two-year struggle with a condition that is causing her body and spirit to waste away. I dealt with it matter-of-factly at first, dragging her to doctors and trusting in their skill to chase away this illness. But there came a time when I began to realize that it was beyond the help of doctors, and that it was out of our control.

Then the terror set in. As I sat in a hospital room, watching her suffer with a nasogastric tube in her throat, needles in her arms, and a hand swollen from infiltrating IV's, I prayed and begged God to intervene. And many times over this struggle, he has, in ways that I could not have expected or ordered, but in the ways that I know are best.

During these days, I find that the depression sometimes paralyzes me. I wake up in the mornings with terror in my heart, and following those fiendish thoughts to their natural conclusion, I imagine worst-possible scenarios and see them as the only possible outcomes. I find it so very difficult to scoop up my fears and lay them in Christ's arms. Though I've written about mothers who've managed to find peace as they took their dread and terror to the Lord, it seems beyond my humanness to follow their example.

So I go to God, my arms full of my ailing daughter and fall to my knees in despair, begging him to give me the strength to do the only thing there is for me to do—lay her in his loving arms, trusting him to answer my prayers and do the things that are best for her, no matter what they might be. And as I weep, the eyes of my heart see his tears, those of a Father weeping for his firstborn. I see the compassion in his eyes, the understanding. I see the brokenheartedness that I have felt. I see that he knows just how I feel. And I realize that God looks at my daughter with as much love as he has for his own Son. More love than I have for her. I can trust him with her.

Mothers and fathers, he loves your children too. And as you deal with the things that happen to them or in them or through them, as you watch the world doing its dirty work on them, as you feel them slipping from your loving grasp, whether voluntarily or

by some evil scheme of the one who hates them, you can trust God. He, too, saw his child ravaged by darkness, ripped apart by the mortal enemy who had sworn to destroy him, pierced through by pure evil. Jesus' own mother stood watching, too, in hopelessness and despair, wondering how this child who was marked by God's own word for greatness could have come to such a crushing end.

But God had a plan. He conquered that evil, through that very crisis. He used that tragedy for a greater purpose. He raised that child up, whole and perfect. And today that very child sits at his right hand, interceding for you and me … for your child and mine … promising that things do turn out well for those who love him.

I say this as much for myself as I say it for you: Keep your focus on the Lord as you endure those crises. Seek him first. Trust him to understand your pain and your terror. And when you don't know how to relinquish your hold and place your child in his hands, then just go to him, your arms full, and kneel at his feet. He will scoop up both of you and hold you close to his heart.

He will see you through. ❧

DEAR GOD: I release my precious child(ren) into your care. Though I have tried every way I know to protect and defend, my efforts have fallen short of the mark. My children need help and you are the only one who can provide it. Pour out your mercy on us, Lord. Our hope is completely invested in your goodness and grace. AMEN.

Zion said, "The LORD has forsaken me,
    the Lord has forgotten me,"
[The LORD says:]
"Can a woman forget the baby at her
        breast
    and have no compassion on the child
        she has borne?
Though she may forget,
    I will not forget you!"

ISAIAH 49:14–15

Each Detail of Our *Lives*

Do not be anxious about anything, but in everything,
by prayer and petition, with thanksgiving,
present your requests to God. And the peace of God,
which transcends all understanding, will guard your hearts
and your minds in Christ Jesus.

PHILIPPIANS 4:6−7

It was a couple of weeks before Christmas some years ago, when I got a phone call from a woman I'd never met before. Her name was Wanda. She told me that she wanted me to know that she had been praying for me for years and only that morning had learned that her prayers had been answered.

Wanda had read an article about me in our local newspaper

some years before. The article talked of my secular writing career, since this was before I had followed God's call to leave that market. As she read that article, God prompted her to pray for me.

Not only did she pray for me that day, but she put me on her prayer list and began to pray for me frequently over the next few years. Her prayer was that I would give my gifts to the Lord and start writing books that would glorify him. She knew nothing about me, except what was in that article, and had no way of knowing that God had brought me under conviction and was calling me to make a change. She prayed diligently, never expecting to know the outcome of those prayers.

Just a few days before calling me, Wanda had gone into a Christian book store to look for a book to give to her unsaved daughter. She told the clerk that she wanted something that would impact her daughter's life. She liked reading suspense, so she asked if there were any suspense novels with a Christian message that might reach her daughter spiritually. "I know just the thing," the sales clerk said. "She might like Terri Blackstock."

Wanda recognized my name immediately, and as she held one of my books in her hand, she realized that her prayer had been answered. I had given my gift to the

Lord. And in his goodness, he had chosen that day to show her the result of her prayers.

Wanda wanted me to know how grateful she was to God, that in his sovereign foresight, he had called her to pray for the person who would write the book that would someday minister to her daughter!

Wanda's story humbled me and brought me to tears, and reminded me that God has his hand in every little detail of our lives. He orchestrates things for our good and his glory, and all the while we think we have something to do with them.

Oh, if we could only remember this when things seem out of control. We're told to "be anxious for nothing." I don't know about you, but I find that difficult. But if I can remind myself that God is in control, that he hasn't fallen asleep or looked away, and that he's involved in the smallest minutiae of my life—the big things, too—then I will never have reason to worry again.

PRECIOUS FATHER: I'm continually amazed by your careful attention to every detail of my life. I would imagine that you have much greater things to attend, and yet you give priority to my simple needs. I am humbled by your love, and I will praise you and thank you for your goodness as long as I live—and for eternity. AMEN.

---

*G*reat is your love, higher than the heavens;
your faithfulness reaches to the skies.

PSALM 108:4

Ensuring *Success*

I can do everything through him who gives me strength.

PHILIPPIANS 4:13

I was sitting in the Green Room at CBN Headquarters in Virginia Beach, waiting to go on The 700 Club, when God taught me one of those lessons that he often teaches when we least expect it. The producer had just come in and told me that I'd be squeezed on at the end of the program, and that I might get six minutes.

My heart sank, because I wanted so much to give my whole testimony about how God had convicted me to leave my career in the secular market and write only Christian fiction. There were so many miracles God had performed in my life, so many things I wanted the 700 Club viewers to know about. But there was no way I could tell them all about it in six minutes.

The guest coordinator of the show and the executive producer were in the Green Room with me, and when the producer who had delivered the startling news retreated, I looked at the other two and confessed that I was nervous. That was an understatement. The truth was that I was in a state of sheer panic.

Without batting an eye, Jackie, the guest coordinator, began to pray for me. She asked God to remind me that he had brought me here for a reason and he wasn't going to forsake me now. Immediately afterward, the two were called away, and I was left in the room alone.

Instantly, I began to pray again. I asked God not to let Terry Meeuwsen, the interviewer, waste time with fluffy talk about writing and publishing, but that the Lord would give her the exact questions that would move the story forward rapidly enough that I could get out the most important parts of my testimony. I asked him to give me peace about going out there under such tight time constraints. And I asked him to clear my head so that my thoughts and words

would flow smoothly. Then I prayed for the hearts of those viewers who needed to hear what God had done for me.

Peace overwhelmed me. When the producer returned, I was calm. Terry asked pertinent and

intelligent questions that jumped the story forward where it was needed, and I was able to get my testimony out. The interesting thing is that some parts of the story—parts that I might have chosen to leave out—God saw fit to leave in. Terry's questions prompted me to share them.

What was the lesson I learned that day? I learned that when we do anything by our own strength, we entertain the potential for failure. But when we empty ourselves of our own intentions, our own plans, our own goals, God will fill us up with his Holy Spirit. When we're directed by the Creator of the universe, we cannot possibly fail.

God gives us everything we need—Christian friends, teachers, churches, pastors, the Bible. But we can only ensure success—whether it be an interview or salvation itself—when we properly use those tools by asking the Father to guide us, Christ to motivate us, and the Holy Spirit to empower us.

Thanks be to God, through Jesus Christ our Lord, that "he who began a good work in you will carry it on to completion until the day of Christ Jesus" (Philippians 1:6). And thanks to our Father for giving us not just the tools but also the reason and power behind those tools to go along with them. And thanks to God, especially, for giving us the outcome—success, always, pure and divine, the way he designed it. ◦—

> FATHER GOD: I have no strength, no stamina, no endurance—without you! With you, I feel as if I can accomplish anything. Help me never to forget that you are the source of my power and the reason for my success. I would be nothing without you, Lord. Thank you for teaching me to trust in you rather than in myself. Thank you for making me so much more than I could ever be on my own. AMEN.

Commit to the LORD whatever you do,
and your plans will succeed.

PROVERBS 16:3

CITY OF REFUGE

My God, my rock, in whom I take refuge, My shield and
the horn of my salvation, my stronghold and my refuge;
My savior, You save me from violence.

2 SAMUEL 22:3 NASB

I've long been fascinated by the cities of refuge ordained by God
in the Old Testament. So fascinated, in fact, that I designed my
whole "Cape Refuge Series" around the concept. As I read back
over Numbers 35, I'm struck by the picture of Christ we see in
these special cities.

As God divided up the Promised Land for the Israelites, he
ordered them to set aside specific cities so that a person who had
unintentionally killed another could flee there and be safe.

For example, if I killed your cousin, you and all your family would have the right, even the responsibility, to avenge that death by killing me. God told the Israelites that murder polluted the land, and it couldn't be tolerated.

However, our merciful God understood that someone could unintentionally kill another, and that person would not be deserving of death. So he set up these cities of refuge, so that accidental killers could flee from their "blood avengers," or the family members of the deceased. As long as the manslayer got through the gates of the city of refuge, he was safe until he could stand trial. If he then stood trial and was found to have killed the person by accident, he was allowed to live in the city of refuge until the death of the high priest. Then he could return to his home. If he was found guilty of premeditated murder, he would be killed.

Once he made it to the city of refuge and was allowed to stay, it was his responsibility to remain within the gates. If he ever ventured outside those gates, he took his life into his own hands. The "blood avenger" was allowed to kill him without penalty.

As I researched the cities of refuge, I learned that God had spaced them out so that no one ever lived more than thirty miles from one. The Israelites were told to keep the roads to them smooth and straight so that the fleeing person would have no hindrance in getting to safety.

I picture myself, with the blood of sin covering my hands. Satan, my blood avenger, chases me, ready to kill me if he can catch me. I picture myself running, running, away from him, desperate to reach the gate of that City, where I'll find Refuge.

I see myself reaching that gate where salvation waits, lingering just outside it, wanting that sweet peace that the city provides, but fearful of crossing that threshold. I long for the life that waits inside, but fear I will be turned away.

I raise my hand to knock, preparing to make my case …

But the door flies open, and I step inside …

And fall into the arms of Refuge, himself.

I'm granted entrance, safe in the arms of my Savior. But Satan roams around outside, hoping to lure me back out of the city walls, waiting to devour me. But he no longer has power over me, for Christ, my high priest, died to set me free, robbing my blood avenger of his accusation, and acquitting me of guilt. ◡

> HOLY FATHER: I will never be able to offer enough praise for the loving-kindness you've poured out on me. You created me, and then when I stubbornly went my own way, you redeemed me. You became a refuge for me, a place of escape from the enemy of my soul. There you offer me forgiveness and an opportunity to begin again. I thank you, Lord. Your love is more than I could have ever thought or imagined. AMEN.

Be selfcontrolled and alert. Your enemy the devil prowls around like a roaring lion looking for someone to devour.

1 PETER 5:8

My Costly *Pardon*

He saved us, not because of righteous things we had done,
but because of his mercy. He saved us through the washing of
rebirth and renewal by the Holy Spirit.

TITUS 3:5

As a Christian writer, I struggle to balance the message and the story. I don't want to preach to any of my readers, nor do I want to read stories that preach to me. But each time I finish a book, I experience the very real fear that someone will read my book and be spiritually moved without knowing where to go from there. What if they realize something is missing in their lives and fall for a false doctrine that might come along at just the right time—a doctrine that would keep them from walking through the door that leads to salvation?

It's possible. And that's why I include my "Afterwords" at the back of each book—to let you know that there is only one way to God, and that is through Jesus Christ, who is the way, the truth, and the light. There are many counterfeit religions, and they're dressed up in pretty packages, promising great rewards. Some promise license to live as we want; others ask us to think of ourselves as gods. There are religions that tickle our ears through psychics and New Age thinking and those that lead to angel worship and offer "spiritual guides" who seem safe but are, in reality, demonic. Perhaps the most counterfeit religion of all, however, is the one in which you sit in church Sunday after Sunday and tell yourself you're a Christian, when you've never entered into a sacred covenant with Christ, never died to yourself, never lived for Christ, and never borne fruit. All of these counterfeits offer cheap hope, temporary pleasure, shallow fulfillment. They also offer a miserable eternity.

Salvation through Christ is not cheap, temporary, or shallow! It teaches that we must deal with sin—my sin, your sin—and only then can we understand why Christ had to die. Only then can we have the promise—not of feeling good and important and guilt-free and unaccountable while on this earth—but of having abundant life on earth, and eternal life in God's presence. The most wonderful worship experience I've ever had is just a sample of what my everyday life will be like in heaven!

But I'm like a prisoner on death row who's been pardoned. All I have to do is accept the pardon and walk out. I have a choice. Why would I deny a pardon that came at such a high price—in fact, at the cost of someone else's life—and insist on finishing out my sentence? I don't know. But day after day, millions and millions of people choose to do just that.

Don't be one of them.

Tell Christ you accept that pardon today, and walk out of your prison into freedom. And if you've already done that, tell someone else, so that they can be pardoned too. ⌒

HEAVENLY FATHER: *My pardon was bought with the blood of your Son. How precious it is! Help me to properly value it, never letting it become mundane or commonplace in my experience. May I spend my life searching for new ways to thank you and walk in the freedom you've provided for me. You are my everything!* AMEN.

he Spirit of the Sovereign LORD is on
    me,
    because the LORD has anointed me
    to preach good news to the poor.
He has sent me to bind up the
        brokenhearted,
    to proclaim freedom for the captives
    and release from darkness for the
        prisoners.

ISAIAH 61:1

or God so loved the world
    that he gave his one and only Son,
that whoever believes in him shall not perish
    but have eternal life.

JOHN 3:16

$\mathcal{T}$o him who is able to keep you from falling

and to present you before his glorious presence without fault

and with great joy—to the only God our savior be glory,

majesty, power and authority, through Jesus Christ our Lord,

before all ages, now and forevermore. Amen.

❧

JUDE 1:24–25

At Inspirio we love to hear from you—
your stories, your feedback,
and your product ideas.
Please send your comments to us
by way of email at
icares@zondervan.com
or to the address below:

inspirio

Attn: Inspirio Cares
5300 Patterson Avenue SE
Grand Rapids, MI 49530

If you would like further information
about Inspirio and the products we
create please visit us at:
www.inspiriogifts.com

Thank you and God bless!

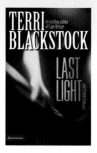

LAST LIGHT

Today, the world as you know it will end.

No need to turn off the lights.

Your car suddenly stalls and won't restart.

You can't call for help because your cell phone is dead.

Everyone around you is having the same problem . . . and it's just the tip of the iceberg.

Your city is in a blackout. Communication is cut off. Hospital equipment won't operate. And airplanes are falling from the sky.

Is it a terrorist attack . . . or something far worse?

In the face of a crisis that sweeps an entire high-tech planet back to the age before electricity, Deni Branning's career ambitions have vanished. She's not about to let her dream of marriage go as well.

But keeping it alive will require extraordinary measures. Yesterday's world is gone. All Deni and her family have left is each other and their neighbors. Their little community will either stand or fall together. But they're only beginning to realize it—and trust doesn't come easily.

Particularly when one of them is a killer.

#1 Bestselling Author of Cape Refuge

Bestselling suspense author Terri Blackstock weaves a masterful what-if novel in which global catastrophe reveals the darkness in human hearts—and lights the way to restoration for a self-centered world.

TERRI BLACKSTOCK (www.terriblackstock.com) is the #1 bestselling author of the Cape Refuge, Sun Coast Chronicles, Second Chances, and Newpointe 911 suspense series, and other books. With Beverly LaHaye, she wrote Seasons Under Heaven, Times and Seasons, Showers in Season, and Season of Blessing.

US $14.99/UK £8.99/CAN $20.99   FICTION / GENERAL / SUSPENSE   ISBN 0-310-25767-0